The measurements inside this book are based on the skeletons of Thomas, Stan and Sue. Many thanks to the Natural History Museum in Los Angeles and the Sedgwick Museum in Cambridge for their help in checking my Tyrannosaurus facts.

To all my wonderful friends, thank you for being there. AL x

First published in North America in 2018 by Boxer Books Limited.
www.boxerbooks.com

Boxer® is a registered trademark of Boxer Books Limited.

Library of Congress Cataloging–in–Publication Data available.

The illustrations were prepared using lino cuts and collagraphs with digital color.
The text is set in Futura.

ISBN 978-1-910716-57-1

1 3 5 7 9 10 8 6 4 2

Printed in China

All of our papers are sourced from managed forests and renewable resources.

HOW TALL
WAS A
T.REX?

ALISON LIMENTANI

BOXER BOOKS

A T. rex might have been
scaly like a reptile,

or feathered like a bird.

Its eyes were as big as baseballs.

baseball   cricket   tennis   pool   golf

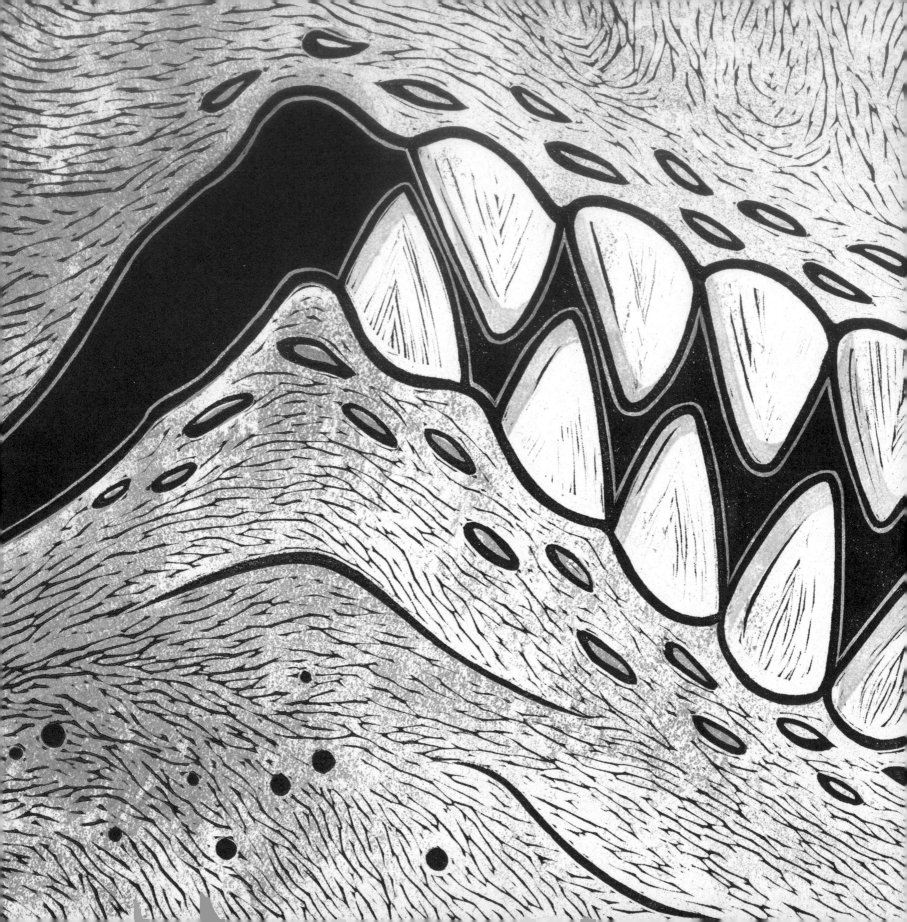

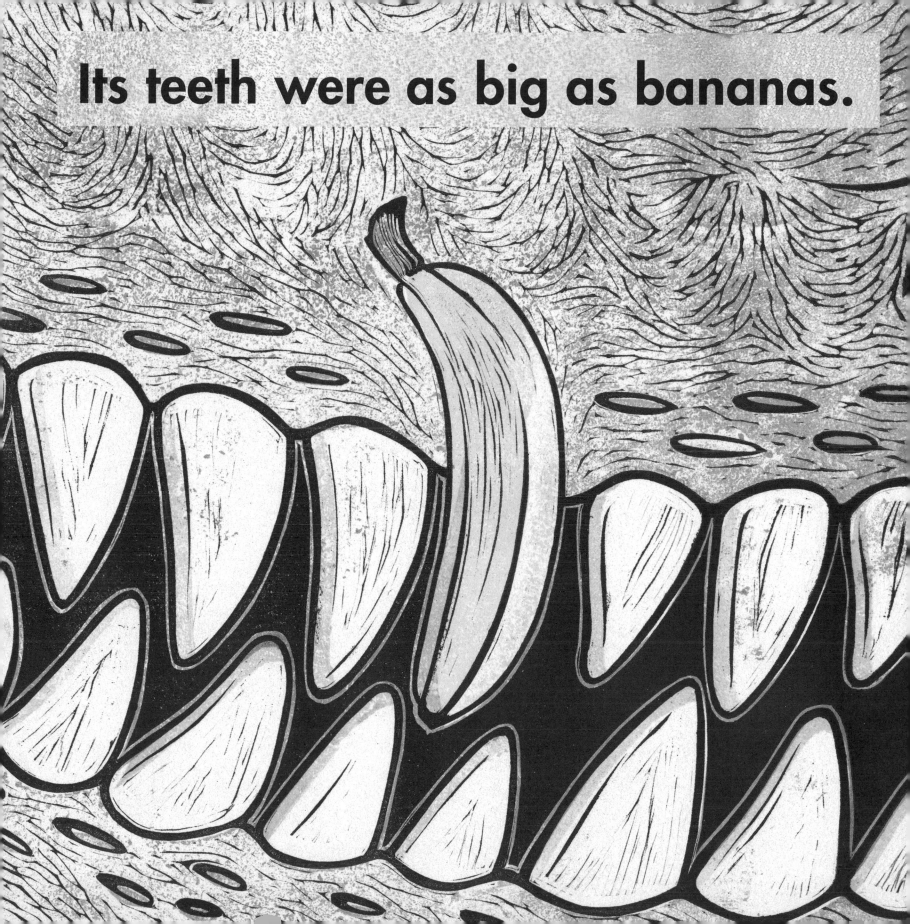

Its teeth were as big as bananas.

A T. rex could have eaten a goat in one gulp!

It was as heavy as 3 hippos.

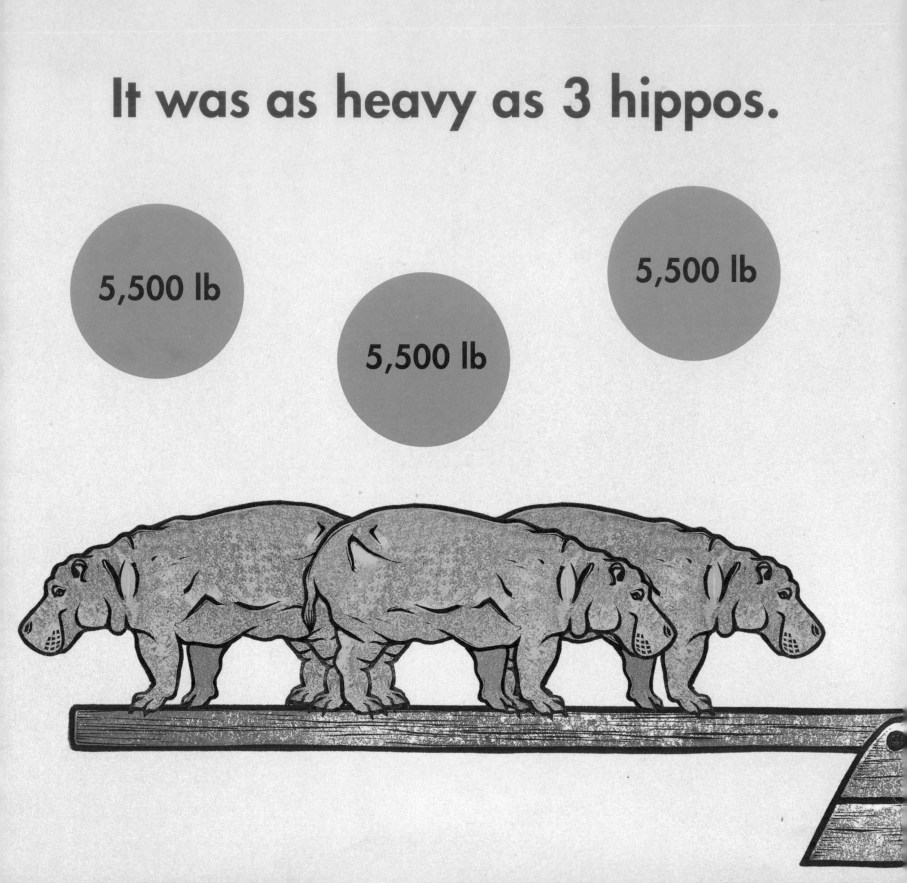

And as long as 6 lions.

A T. rex could have run as fast as an elephant or a meerkat,

10–25 mph

70 mph

but slower than a cheetah.

37 children's footprints could fit inside one T. rex footprint!

But how tall was a T. rex?

A T. rex was as tall as
10 velociraptors.

Or half as tall as
a brachiosaurus.

Or as tall as a giraffe!

Scientists can tell a lot about dinosaurs by looking at bones and fossils. The facts in this book are based on what we currently think about the Tyrannosaurus rex, but who knows what we'll discover in the future!

Skull length = up to 4.76 ft

Eye sockets = up to 4.7 in

Tooth length = up to 9.8 in

Head to tail length = up to 39 ft

Height to hips = up to 13 ft
(Total reach estimated at 16.4 ft)

Height = 12–20 in

Height = 29–49 ft

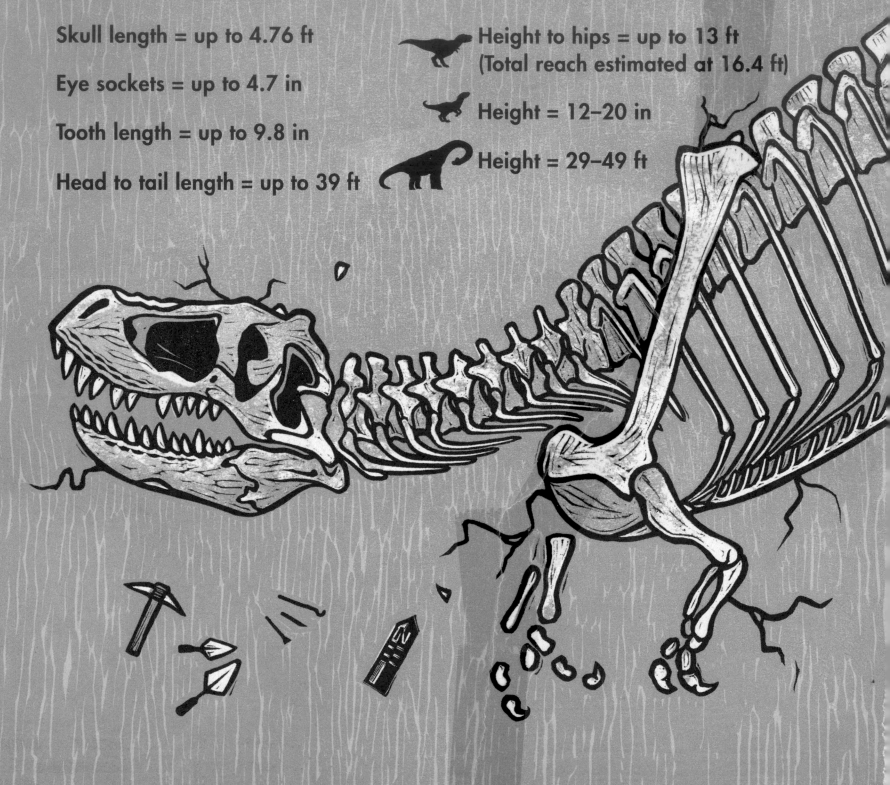